8 WEEKS TOWARDS ACCEPTANCE

8 Weeks Towards **ACCEPTANCE**

A guided journal to help you accept and adapt to life as you know it

KATY SHERIDAN

ISBN: 978-1-9163500-2-1

Further resources, information, podcasts and training are available from Maximum Edge CIC – a community interest company based in the UK, specialising in the development of people, with the aim of strengthening communities.

Website: www.maximumedge.org.uk
X (Twitter): @MaxEdgeCIC
Instagram: @maxedgecic
Facebook: @MaxEdgeCIC
YouTube: Maximum Edge CIC

For audio content, ask your smart-speaker to "play Maximum Edge CIC Podcast Channel" or find our channel on Podbean and podcast streaming channels

10 9 8 7 6 5 4 3 2 1

CONTENTS

The most terrifying thing is to accept oneself completely.

CARL JUNG, PSYCHIATRIST

INTRODUCTION

There are choices we make which affect our whole outlook on life.

We all tend to forget about the little things and focus on the big things in life. Big changes, big worries (or lots of little worries), big goals. It can be great to 'think big' but forgetting about the little things in life doesn't allow us to appreciate all the achievements we make every day - or to be grateful for the things and people we have around us.

This 8-week journal gives you a place to record those goals and achievements, change habits, challenge yourself and ultimately feel more accepting, more often.

Writing things down helps us to de-clutter our minds and gain some clarity from the ongoing thoughts which can take over our waking lives. Seeing our thoughts on paper can give us clarity and help us identify what it is we really want.

The next step would be to share these goals and dreams with people we trust, but for now, this journal is your stepping-stone to a more accepting you.

Things to remember:

1. This is *your* book.
2. Nobody needs to see it.
3. Your writing doesn't need to be perfect.
4. You can make mistakes.
5. You might miss the odd day.

Take pressure off yourself and use this journal as your kick-start towards a *More Accepting You*.

WHAT IS ACCEPTANCE?

Definitions include:

- The process of recognising something as valid or correct
- Being at peace with a decision made
- A willingness to live with, or adapt to, a given circumstance
- A person's agreement to a particular reality, without attempting to change it or object to it
- Surrendering your expectations of something or someone, without judgement
- Seeing reality as it is right now

Acceptance can be applied to:

- Circumstances and situations which occur/have occurred
- Other people
- Aspects of yourself
- Values, Beliefs and Opinions

WHY IS ACCEPTANCE SO IMPORTANT?

Without acceptance, we live in a constant battle with others, situations and ourselves. It creates physical and mental stress, putting us at greater risk of anxiety, depression, high blood pressure, sleep problems, memory and focus issues, physical tension and feelings of anger, frustration and hopelessness.

Maybe you don't have the energy, resources or willpower to do anything about a situation at the moment, but by accepting it, you are one step closer to making those changes, because once we accept something, we can really *see* it and decide on our next move.

WHERE MIGHT YOU NEED TO PRACTISE ACCEPTANCE?

Maybe someone you know has always behaved a certain way with you, and you really wish they didn't do and say the things they say. You might have tried talking to them about it or you might not - but if they have behaved in a certain way for a long time, it's unlikely that they will ever stop doing it. Would it not be better if you could instead accept that this is the way they are *for now*?

It could be that your health is deteriorating, and you can no longer enjoy a sport which you once loved playing. Maybe you try to deny your health problems and carry on anyway, causing physical pain and mental stress. Or perhaps you watch your team play, but inside you feel angry and envious that you can no longer be on the pitch. Would it not be better if you could instead accept that this is the way you are *for now*?

Perhaps you are struggling to make ends meet, financially. Are you comparing yourself to other people, or to a previous version of yourself? Would it not be better if you could instead accept that this is the way things are *for now*?

IF YOU ACCEPT SOMETHING, ARE YOU JUST GIVING IN?

The answer to this question depends on your approach - your *mindset*.

To fully accept something is to truly see it, without any emotion or judgement attached to it. Through this process, we are given the space and time we need to make lasting changes in our lives.

By accepting something/someone/aspects of ourself, we give ourselves permission to stop fighting, to listen more, to relax.

WHY CAN ACCEPTANCE BE SO DIFFICULT?

There is only ONE you.

You are the only person who has the feelings you have, when you have them, caused by whoever or whatever caused them.

That doesn't mean nobody else experiences the same feelings as you. What it means is: *only you* react to a particular person, event or experience your way, *only you* have your particular set of memories - and emotions attached to them and *only you* want the things you want, the way you want them.

There is nothing wrong with expecting kindness, respect and honesty but it is unrealistic, and ultimately unfair, to expect others to feel, think or behave the same as us, all the time. Are they not just behaving in a way that makes them... *them?*

Other peoples' behaviour, way of life, attitudes, beliefs, clothing, relationships (and more) challenge us, simply because they are **not** us. Similarly, certain aspects of our *own* personality can make us feel uncomfortable, by reminding us of previous experiences, or of the way people around us have behaved in the past. All these things can trigger negative thoughts and feelings inside us, including a lack of worth, jealousy, anger, belittlement, loneliness or sometimes just a general feeling of being emotionally worn out.

Acceptance challenges us, which is why it can be so difficult. It takes us out of our comfort zone.

We may have been trying to change or object to people, situations, emotions, and feelings which we don't accept, for *so* long, that the thought of NOT trying to change or object to it any longer is a real genuine challenge.

But you are ready for that challenge. That is why you have this journal.

If you don't like something, change it.
If you can't change it, change your attitude.

MAYA ANJELOU, AUTHOR

IDENTIFYING WHAT WE DON'T ACCEPT

There are many things which we may not accept; aspects and behaviours of other people; situations you find yourself in; events which have happened; traits of your own personality. Sometimes it is us looking out at others and sometimes we are looking in at ourselves. Some things may be huge global issues while others may be very personal to us.

Here is a list to get you thinking about things which maybe you don't accept:

- You are at risk of redundancy
- Climate change is affecting our way of life
- People think you are attractive
- You have had a health diagnosis
- You partner doesn't listen to what you want
- You are wrong
- Your employer wants you to change your hours or conditions
- The relationship between two people you know
- You are a creative person
- A person you love has died
- Local building plans on green belt fields near your home
- A relationship has ended, or is about to
- You have put on weight and don't feel good
- Discrimination of some kind e.g. racism, sexism
- You could be good at learning a new skill
- You lost
- You sometimes have bad days when you don't want to get up
- Someone in your life makes you feel very negative
- Your grown-up child is ready to leave home
- You have less money than you had in the past

Now it is your turn. Turn to the next page and *be honest….*

TASK 1: IDENTIFY WHAT YOU DON'T ACCEPT

Make a list of *everything* which you find hard to accept. Note them in the table. There is no need for any specific details at this point.

It could be anything, anyone or any aspect of yourself – everything and everyone which you would secretly like to just say **no** to (and maybe you already have).

Situations which occur/have occurred that I do not accept
People who I do not accept
Aspects of myself which I do not accept
Values, Beliefs and Opinions which I do not accept
Other things which I do not accept

(Continue on more paper if required)

WHEEL OF ACCEPTANCE

Now is a good time to review where you are in your life. Be truthful about how accepting you are and how much you are 'fighting'.

A tool we can use to do this is the Wheel of Acceptance. You will find a blank wheel opposite which, once completed, will give you an indication of the areas of your life which you may choose to work on over the next 8 weeks.

The 5 sections of the Wheel represent different areas of acceptance.

- Score your level of acceptance on each category out of 10 by drawing a line to create a new outer edge (see example below). Use the centre of the wheel as 0 - *totally unaccepting* and the outer edge as 10 - *completely accepting*
- Note that very few people will mark 10 on all - or any - of their categories. This would indicate that they are fully accepting of every situation, every belief, every person they come across and every aspect of themself, which is unrealistic.
- When you have completed the wheel, the new shape represents your Wheel of Acceptance. You should be able to see the areas in your life which you struggle to accept.
- This is your starting point from today.

Example

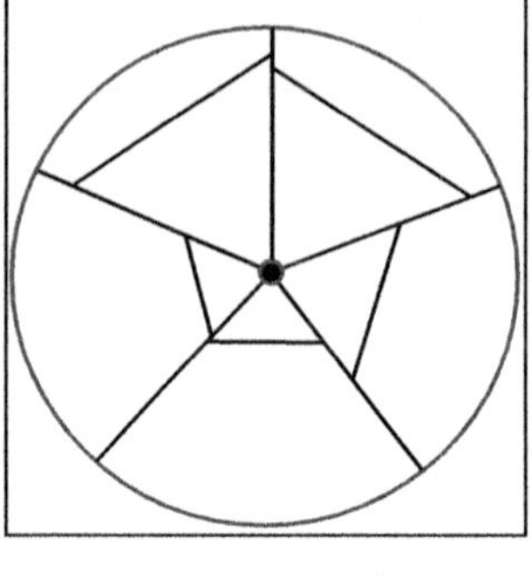

MY WHEEL OF ACCEPTANCE

COMPLETED ON:_______________

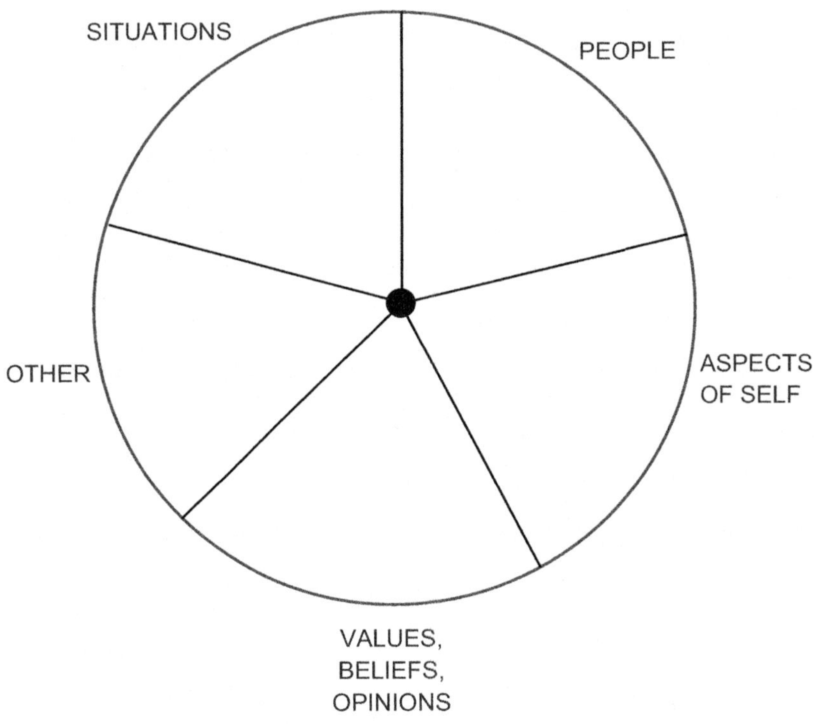

THE BATTLE (WHAT IF WE CAN'T ACCEPT IT?)

The opposite of acceptance is rejection, defined as:

Denial, Avoidance, Repression, Exclusion (D.A.R.E.)

When we look at those words, all of them have negative implications for us and our health. We end up in a constant battle with ourselves about how to deny the existence of something, avoid a situation or a person, repress feelings attached to a situation or person, and exclude something/someone from our life.

The following examples show us what the battle is, why we can't accept it and the impact that battle can have on us:

The Battle	The Reason	The impact
Denying your health is deteriorating	*Accepting* it might mean you have to give things up which you enjoy	You ignore health advice, causing more damage in the future
Denying that you are good at something	To explore it further would mean leaving your comfort zone	You don't experience the joy which comes with achieving new things
Avoiding a particular person	They make you feel very negative	Constant thought about where you may see them, what you will do or say if they approach or contact you, how you can avoid them (in person/online)
Avoiding all the news	It makes you so worried, angry or sad	You miss out on current affairs and the *good* news which can be found if you look in the right places

Repressing asking for what you want	You think the other person won't understand or may laugh at you	You feel irritated, resentful and unfulfilled
Repressing your longing to be with someone or to do something you love	You think other people would no longer accept *you*	Feeling heartache, longing and frustration
Excluding someone from events	They always embarrass you and you don't want to feel like that again	You feel guilty, devious and unkind
Excluding a hobby from your life	it causes a rift in your relationship	You feel anger, resentment and bitterness

From the central column (The Reason), you can see there are some valid reasons *why* we don't accept some things. We use it as a way to protect ourselves from hurt. But by keeping these battles going, we live in a constant state of negativity towards situations, people or aspects of ourselves that we just cannot accept.

When we look at the third column, we see all the destructive feelings attached to each battle and now start to become more aware of how much our lack of acceptance affects our day to day thought processes.

Constant sources of negativity have consequences for our mental and physical health - and can cause problems in our close relationships if we are always trying to change or object to situations and people which we do not accept.

TASK 2: DO YOU D.A.R.E?

Take another look at your completed table on Task 1 ("Identify what you don't accept"*)*, and using the following key, put one or more letter(s) next to each item in your table related to your battles:

D = Deny **A** = Avoid **R** = Repress **E** = Exclude

Can you see how much energy you are using by trying to deny, avoid, repress or exclude these things, feelings or people from your life?

TASK 3: MY BATTLE LIST

You will have your own battles which you fight; and may have fought for a long time. Have a go at completing the following table using an issue you identified in Task 1 against the rejections of Task 2

The Battle	The Reason I do this is because:	The impact on me is:
eg: I avoid seeing my brother	eg: he makes me feel so negative	eg: constantly thinking about where he may be, what I will do or say if I see him (in person or online)

1. I deny…

2. I avoid…

3. I repress…

4. I exclude…

(NOTE: do this task for everything in Task 1 when you have time)

You have now identified what you cannot accept – and figured out the ways in which you reject them.

GRIEVING WHAT COULD HAVE BEEN

To accept is also to give ourselves space and time to *grieve* something which has gone; or has never been. It is important that you take as long as you need to in this part of the process, to address your feelings of loss.

You may have been placing so many expectations on a person or situation for so long and as a result, you may have been let down repeatedly when your expectations have not been met.

Grief is often misunderstood to only apply to bereavement. But grief can be applied to *any* loss in our life, including the *concept* of loss, for something that has never been or will never be. For example:

- If we lose our job, we grieve until we feel ready to move on to applying for other positions.
- If we become ill, we grieve our health and what that means for our immediate and long-term future.
- If we lose our freedom (for example lockdown), we grieve it, until we identify what we *can* do, not what we *can't* do.
- If a relationship ends, we grieve the feelings that person gave us and the possibilities of what could have been, until we are ready to look for different opportunities on our own or with others.

Some more examples of grief are:

- The sportsperson who can no longer play can grieve their fitness.
- The daughter who wanted an affectionate mother can grieve their love.
- The woman who is childless can grieve a motherhood.
- The artist who didn't enter a piece of work into a competition can grieve the lost opportunity.
- The employee who never gets the promotion can grieve the luxury life they had envisioned.

Grief is a process, with stages to go through. The most widely agreed stages are:

shock > *denial* > *bargaining* > *guilt* > *frustration* >

depression > *experimentation* > *acceptance*

Shock that this is real and happening

Denial that it will just be for a week or two and then everything will be back to 'normal'. Act as if nothing has happened and feel more energised

Bargaining that we could find a workaround, for example "if they want me to do *x* for them, I don't have time for *y* *as*well." Or "If she's going to keep making me feel worthless, I'll do the same to her".

Guilt that you feel you have may have somehow caused this to happen, or could have prevented it

Frustration that it has happened and it all seems so unfair

Depression that we will never get back to life as we knew it

Experimentation of different ways of living with the new situation

Acceptance that it has happened, we will do our best to go through it, and can see a brighter future

It is only at the point of acceptance that we can begin to shine as employees, parents, carers, friends, siblings, sons, daughters, partners, and we begin to realise that there is a future ahead. It may look different to how we originally wanted it, but we will make the most of what we *do* have, and not dwell on what we *don't*.

However, we cannot get to acceptance without first going through the other seven stages.

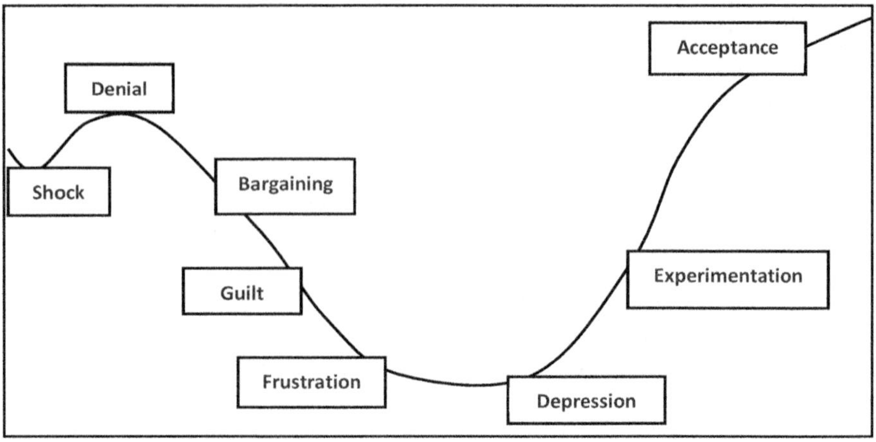

The Stages of Grief (inspired by the original Kubler-Ross model). The whole process is rarely straightforward, with feelings often swaying from one to the other and back again.

Depending on many factors, including your commitment, the stages could take from a few moments in deep thought – to many weeks and months, involving professional help. But there is *always* acceptance at the end, after which *you* are in control, and *you* shape what comes next.

THE IMPORTANCE OF SELF-ACCEPTANCE

No two people share the same life, values, relationships, memories, emotions, upbringing, health, personality and history. We are all different.

For me, the penny dropped from one comment I made with a group of friends: "I'm not creative.". There was an exclaimed chorus of "Yes you are!" and a conversation followed about all the things I had done to convince these people otherwise. The question was - Why didn't I accept this about *myself*? What was causing me to believe I wasn't creative?

If I accepted that I *was* creative, what opportunities could come my way which I would previously have turned down, believing that I just wasn't creative enough to do them? My head was swimming.

There may be traits about yourself which you absolutely believe to be true. For example, you are not funny or clever or good looking or rich enough, or that you are just not *enough*. Or you are too loud, too bossy, too quiet, too focused or just *too much*.

Is there a particular trait you feel you don't possess? Something which you believe other people are so much better at than you? Something which, given the chance, you would love to do more of or learn more about? Maybe it's something you enjoyed as a child but wouldn't dream of having a go at now. Something which has held you back because you just don't have enough self-belief to try (or try again).

Have a look at your answers in TASK 1, and consider them with an approach of acceptance...

Maybe instead of feeling like an outsider or loner, and not fitting in, you can start to see yourself as a thinker, a watcher, someone who is observant, patient, and a good listener. Or if you think your work isn't good enough, ask yourself why you think that. Are you comparing your work to others? (see next section)

By understanding ourselves more, we can accept who we are now – and start to plan a life ahead **with** all our personal history, feelings, quirks and features instead of trying to reject those parts of ourselves.

COMPARING OURSELVES

Many of our beliefs about ourselves come from comparing ourselves to others, and to ourselves at a different time in our lives.

Today, comparison to others is almost inescapable. From the minute we wake up to the moment we go to bed, we are bombarded with images, stories, memes, videos, messages and adverts of others. They make us stop and think about ourselves, wondering if we should be looking like, sounding like, wearing, talking, doing, dancing like the other people we see and hear.

In addition to this, we compare our current self with a past version of ourself. The one who went out a lot. The one who laughed more. The one who was successful at dating. The one who was adventurous. The one who could paint or dance or sing. The one who earned lots of money. The one who owned their own house. The one who had a daughter or grandma or cat.

By comparing ourselves with others and our previous 'self', we are not fully living in the present. We are living in a state of jealousy, frustration, or sadness, and over time this can cause our bodies to be in a permanent state of stress, with symptoms of tension, insomnia, depression and anxiety.

By comparing ourselves less, we can start to accept what we *have* instead of what we *don't* have, and starting at the very base level, you have your life. Is it time to start living it more?

ACCEPTING OTHERS

People generally don't intend to hurt those closest to them but often do so unknowingly due to various factors:

- Learned behaviour
- Unresolved personal hurt
- Unawareness of the impact of their actions on others
- Fear of intimacy
- Communication challenges
- Mental health issues
- High stress levels

Understanding these reasons can help us comprehend their behaviour as not reflecting us, but of them. While expressing how we feel to someone who has hurt us can be beneficial, it's important to consider how our words may affect them. Expecting immediate change or a permanent apology may not be realistic.

Might it be better to accept what has happened, accept that they may hurt you again and accept them for who and what they are now? If they change in the future and give you a heartfelt apology that would be incredible. Unlikely but incredible.

In TASK 1 "People I do not accept" - think back to how the person was when you first met. Have they changed? Has something happened to them which has had an impact on how they behave? Are they likely to change again? Have *you* changed?

Once we accept a person for who, what, and how they are now, we can slow down the fight inside and start to plan a way forward with empathy and understanding for them. This doesn't mean we condone bad behaviour in others, but by identifying what exactly we don't accept in them, we can make a conscious decision to move on, with or without them in our lives, by setting clear boundaries and prioritising our own wellbeing.

HOW TO USE THIS JOURNAL

Choose a time in your day when you are going to use your journal. You might want to try different times to find out when suits you best. First thing in the morning or last thing at night often work well. As long as you are not too tired and won't be distracted, you can use your journal whenever you want. If you choose to complete the journal in the morning, you can reflect on the day before whilst focusing on your tasks ahead.

You will find a new section for each week, plus a 4 weekly review and an 8-week reflection. If you miss a couple of days don't worry about it! Just get back on track as soon as you can.

You have space each day to plan and reflect on what that day has given you, and what you have achieved.

At the start of each week set your goal. Breaking large goals down into manageable tasks makes them more achievable over time.

If you can't think of something to write, there is no pressure to complete every section every day, but once you get into the habit of stopping and thinking, you will probably surprise yourself with how much of it you *can* complete.

There is space every day for you to add your own notes to make this journal entirely your own, and there is also a To Do list area. However, use this with caution! Don't let it become your day-to-day list of jobs that need doing, people you need to email etc. Keep it brief and specifically focused on that week's goals.

When we invest so much of our energy in denying, avoiding, repressing or excluding things from our life, it can come as something of a shock to suddenly embrace, accept, even *encourage* something or someone which has caused us pain in the past.

But you are ready, so…

BEGIN

WEEK 1: CHOOSE YOUR GOAL

Choose one item from TASK 1 which you want to address. Tick which type it is, then briefly write what it is in the box below.

□ Situation □ Person □ Aspect of Myself □ Value/Belief/Opinion

Write down the way(s) in which you DARE it by Denying, Avoiding, Repressing, or Excluding

I DENY this when I…	I AVOID this when I…
I REPRESS this when I…	I EXCLUDE this when I…

Dissect the details of *why* you can't accept this person/situation. Continue on more paper if you need to.

Grieve the expectations you had about this situation, person or aspect of yourself. You may want to write notes down here. Remember: it's normal to also feel grief for something you've never had or can never have.

Decide to fully accept some or all aspects of this situation/person/ aspect of yourself from today onwards, until you are ready to do things differently.:

Plan to move forward without letting it affect you negatively anymore.

To help me with this, I may need to:

Monday **Date:**

Overall I am feeling: 1 2 3 4 5 6 7 8 9 10

Through acceptance, I realise:

For self-care, I will / I did:

Going forward, I choose to:

Tuesday

Overall I am feeling: 1 2 3 4 5 6 7 8 9 10

Through acceptance, I realise:

For self-care, I will / I did:

Going forward, I choose to:

Wednesday

Overall I am feeling: 1 2 3 4 5 6 7 8 9 10

Through acceptance, I realise:

For self-care, I will / I did:

Going forward, I choose to:

Thursday

Overall I am feeling: 1 2 3 4 5 6 7 8 9 10

Through acceptance, I realise: ____________________

For self-care, I will / I did: ____________________

Going forward, I choose to: ____________________

Friday

Overall I am feeling: 1 2 3 4 5 6 7 8 9 10

Through acceptance, I realise: ____________________

For self-care, I will / I did: ____________________

Going forward, I choose to: ____________________

Saturday

Overall I am feeling: 1 2 3 4 5 6 7 8 9 10

Through acceptance, I realise: ____________________

For self-care, I will / I did: ____________________

Going forward, I choose to: ____________________

Sunday

Overall I am feeling: 1 2 3 4 5 6 7 8 9 10

Through acceptance, I realise:

For self-care, I will / I did:

Going forward, I choose to:

My notes:

When you accept others as they are, you give them the freedom to be themselves.

UNKNOWN

WEEK 2: CHOOSE YOUR GOAL

Choose one item from TASK 1 which you want to address. Tick which type it is, then briefly write what it is in the box below.

□ Situation □ Person □ Aspect of Myself □ Value/Belief/Opinion

Write down the way(s) in which you DARE it by Denying, Avoiding, Repressing, or Excluding

I DENY this when I…	I AVOID this when I…
I REPRESS this when I…	I EXCLUDE this when I…

Dissect the details of *why* you can't accept this person/situation. Continue on more paper if you need to.

Grieve the expectations you had about this situation, person or aspect of yourself. You may want to write notes down here. Remember: it's normal to also feel grief for something you've never had or can never have.

Decide to fully accept some or all aspects of this situation/person/ aspect of yourself from today onwards, until you are ready to do things differently.:

Plan to move forward without letting it affect you negatively anymore.

To help me with this, I may need to:

Monday **Date:**

Overall I am feeling: 1 2 3 4 5 6 7 8 9 10

Through acceptance, I realise:

For self-care, I will / I did:

Going forward, I choose to:

Tuesday

Overall I am feeling: 1 2 3 4 5 6 7 8 9 10

Through acceptance, I realise:

For self-care, I will / I did:

Going forward, I choose to:

Wednesday

Overall I am feeling: 1 2 3 4 5 6 7 8 9 10

Through acceptance, I realise:

For self-care, I will / I did:

Going forward, I choose to:

Thursday

Overall I am feeling: 1 2 3 4 5 6 7 8 9 10

Through acceptance, I realise:

For self-care, I will / I did:

Going forward, I choose to:

Friday

Overall I am feeling: 1 2 3 4 5 6 7 8 9 10

Through acceptance, I realise:

For self-care, I will / I did:

Going forward, I choose to:

Saturday

Overall I am feeling: 1 2 3 4 5 6 7 8 9 10

Through acceptance, I realise:

For self-care, I will / I did:

Going forward, I choose to:

Sunday

Overall I am feeling: 1 2 3 4 5 6 7 8 9 10

Through acceptance, I realise: ______________________

For self-care, I will / I did: ______________________

Going forward, I choose to: ______________________

My notes: ______________________

The greatest gift that you can give to others
is the gift of unconditional love and acceptance.

BRIAN TRACY, MOTIVATIONAL SPEAKER

WEEK 3: CHOOSE YOUR GOAL

Choose one item from TASK 1 which you want to address. Tick which type it is, then briefly write what it is in the box below.

□ Situation □ Person □ Aspect of Myself □ Value/Belief/Opinion

Write down the way(s) in which you DARE it by Denying, Avoiding, Repressing, or Excluding

I DENY this when I…	I AVOID this when I…
I REPRESS this when I…	I EXCLUDE this when I…

Dissect the details of *why* you can't accept this person/situation. Continue on more paper if you need to.

Grieve the expectations you had about this situation, person or aspect of yourself. You may want to write notes down here. Remember: it's normal to also feel grief for something you've never had or can never have.

Decide to fully accept some or all aspects of this situation/person/ aspect of yourself from today onwards, until you are ready to do things differently.:

Plan to move forward without letting it affect you negatively anymore.

To help me with this, I may need to:

Monday **Date:**

Overall I am feeling: 1 2 3 4 5 6 7 8 9 10

Through acceptance, I realise:

For self-care, I will / I did:

Going forward, I choose to:

Tuesday

Overall I am feeling: 1 2 3 4 5 6 7 8 9 10

Through acceptance, I realise:

For self-care, I will / I did:

Going forward, I choose to:

Wednesday

Overall I am feeling: 1 2 3 4 5 6 7 8 9 10

Through acceptance, I realise:

For self-care, I will / I did:

Going forward, I choose to:

Thursday

Overall I am feeling: 1 2 3 4 5 6 7 8 9 10

Through acceptance, I realise:

For self-care, I will / I did:

Going forward, I choose to:

Friday

Overall I am feeling: 1 2 3 4 5 6 7 8 9 10

Through acceptance, I realise:

For self-care, I will / I did:

Going forward, I choose to:

Saturday

Overall I am feeling: 1 2 3 4 5 6 7 8 9 10

Through acceptance, I realise:

For self-care, I will / I did:

Going forward, I choose to:

Sunday

Overall I am feeling: 1 2 3 4 5 6 7 8 9 10

Through acceptance, I realise:

For self-care, I will / I did:

Going forward, I choose to:

My notes:

Happiness can only exist in acceptance.

GEORGE ORWELL, AUTHOR

WEEK 4: CHOOSE YOUR GOAL

Choose one item from TASK 1 which you want to address. Tick which type it is, then briefly write what it is in the box below.

□ Situation □ Person □ Aspect of Myself □ Value/Belief/Opinion

Write down the way(s) in which you DARE it by Denying, Avoiding, Repressing, or Excluding

I DENY this when I…	I AVOID this when I…
I REPRESS this when I…	I EXCLUDE this when I…

Dissect the details of *why* you can't accept this person/situation. Continue on more paper if you need to.

Grieve the expectations you had about this situation, person or aspect of yourself. You may want to write notes down here. Remember: it's normal to also feel grief for something you've never had or can never have.

Decide to fully accept some or all aspects of this situation/person/ aspect of yourself from today onwards, until you are ready to do things differently.:

Plan to move forward without letting it affect you negatively anymore.

To help me with this, I may need to:

Monday **Date:**

Overall I am feeling: 1 2 3 4 5 6 7 8 9 10

Through acceptance, I realise:

For self-care, I will / I did:

Going forward, I choose to:

Tuesday

Overall I am feeling: 1 2 3 4 5 6 7 8 9 10

Through acceptance, I realise:

For self-care, I will / I did:

Going forward, I choose to:

Wednesday

Overall I am feeling: 1 2 3 4 5 6 7 8 9 10

Through acceptance, I realise:

For self-care, I will / I did:

Going forward, I choose to:

Thursday

Overall I am feeling: 1 2 3 4 5 6 7 8 9 10

Through acceptance, I realise:

For self-care, I will / I did:

Going forward, I choose to:

Friday

Overall I am feeling: 1 2 3 4 5 6 7 8 9 10

Through acceptance, I realise:

For self-care, I will / I did:

Going forward, I choose to:

Saturday

Overall I am feeling: 1 2 3 4 5 6 7 8 9 10

Through acceptance, I realise:

For self-care, I will / I did:

Going forward, I choose to:

Sunday

Overall I am feeling: 1 2 3 4 5 6 7 8 9 10

Through acceptance, I realise:

For self-care, I will / I did:

Going forward, I choose to:

My notes:

HALFWAY THERE

You are halfway there! How do you feel?

Make a point now of looking back to the start of this process and remembering how you felt *then*. Were you excited? Motivated? Daunted?

Have you already made progress in accepting some of the items from your list on Task 1? If you haven't, there are still 4 weeks left, so no need to panic or feel under pressure. You are in control of the goals you have set for yourself.

By now you might have started to notice patterns and triggers in your life which cause you to feel and behave more (and less) accepting than at other times. Be aware of the things which cause you to be less accepting and instead focus on those which cause you to feel positive and to treat others and yourself well. Use this as your encouragement to continue.

How does your body feel? Are you less stressed? Do you sleep better? Can you concentrate for longer? Are you feeling more positive or more confident? Any subtle changes that you are noticing will add up to a more accepting, happier, less stressed you.

Stay focused on the tasks you set. Go back and review them, or alter them for the next four weeks. Maybe set yourself some different ones. It's entirely up to you.

Use this half-way point to look backwards and then to look forwards to the next 4 weeks.

My notes:

CONTINUE

WEEK 5: CHOOSE YOUR GOAL

Choose one item from TASK 1 which you want to address. Tick which type it is, then briefly write what it is in the box below.

□ Situation □ Person □ Aspect of Myself □ Value/Belief/Opinion

Write down the way(s) in which you DARE it by Denying, Avoiding, Repressing, or Excluding

I DENY this when I…	I AVOID this when I…
I REPRESS this when I…	I EXCLUDE this when I…

Dissect the details of *why* you can't accept this person/situation. Continue on more paper if you need to.

<u>Grieve</u> the expectations you had about this situation, person or aspect of yourself. You may want to write notes down here. Remember: it's normal to also feel grief for something you've never had or can never have.

<u>Decide</u> to fully accept some or all aspects of this situation/person/aspect of yourself from today onwards, until you are ready to do things differently.:

<u>Plan</u> to move forward without letting it affect you negatively anymore.

To help me with this, I may need to:

Monday **Date:**

Overall I am feeling: 1 2 3 4 5 6 7 8 9 10

Through acceptance, I realise:

For self-care, I will / I did:

Going forward, I choose to:

Tuesday

Overall I am feeling: 1 2 3 4 5 6 7 8 9 10

Through acceptance, I realise:

For self-care, I will / I did:

Going forward, I choose to:

Wednesday

Overall I am feeling: 1 2 3 4 5 6 7 8 9 10

Through acceptance, I realise:

For self-care, I will / I did:

Going forward, I choose to:

Thursday

Overall I am feeling: 1 2 3 4 5 6 7 8 9 10

Through acceptance, I realise:

For self-care, I will / I did:

Going forward, I choose to:

Friday

Overall I am feeling: 1 2 3 4 5 6 7 8 9 10

Through acceptance, I realise:

For self-care, I will / I did:

Going forward, I choose to:

Saturday

Overall I am feeling: 1 2 3 4 5 6 7 8 9 10

Through acceptance, I realise:

For self-care, I will / I did:

Going forward, I choose to:

Sunday

Overall I am feeling: 1 2 3 4 5 6 7 8 9 10

Through acceptance, I realise: __________

For self-care, I will / I did: __________

Going forward, I choose to: __________

My notes: __________

When I accept myself, I am freed from the burden of needing you to accept me.

STEVE MARABOLI, AUTHOR

WEEK 6: CHOOSE YOUR GOAL

Choose one item from TASK 1 which you want to address. Tick which type it is, then briefly write what it is in the box below.

□ Situation □ Person □ Aspect of Myself □ Value/Belief/Opinion

Write down the way(s) in which you DARE it by Denying, Avoiding, Repressing, or Excluding

I DENY this when I...	I AVOID this when I...
I REPRESS this when I...	I EXCLUDE this when I...

Dissect the details of *why* you can't accept this person/situation. Continue on more paper if you need to.

Grieve the expectations you had about this situation, person or aspect of yourself. You may want to write notes down here. Remember: it's normal to also feel grief for something you've never had or can never have.

Decide to fully accept some or all aspects of this situation/person/ aspect of yourself from today onwards, until you are ready to do things differently.:

Plan to move forward without letting it affect you negatively anymore.

To help me with this, I may need to:

Monday **Date:**

Overall I am feeling: 1 2 3 4 5 6 7 8 9 10

Through acceptance, I realise:

For self-care, I will / I did:

Going forward, I choose to:

Tuesday

Overall I am feeling: 1 2 3 4 5 6 7 8 9 10

Through acceptance, I realise:

For self-care, I will / I did:

Going forward, I choose to:

Wednesday

Overall I am feeling: 1 2 3 4 5 6 7 8 9 10

Through acceptance, I realise:

For self-care, I will / I did:

Going forward, I choose to:

Thursday

Overall I am feeling: 1 2 3 4 5 6 7 8 9 10

Through acceptance, I realise:

For self-care, I will / I did:

Going forward, I choose to:

Friday

Overall I am feeling: 1 2 3 4 5 6 7 8 9 10

Through acceptance, I realise:

For self-care, I will / I did:

Going forward, I choose to:

Saturday

Overall I am feeling: 1 2 3 4 5 6 7 8 9 10

Through acceptance, I realise:

For self-care, I will / I did:

Going forward, I choose to:

Sunday

Overall I am feeling: 1 2 3 4 5 6 7 8 9 10

Through acceptance, I realise:

For self-care, I will / I did:

Going forward, I choose to:

My notes:

If you're walking down the right path and you're willing to keep walking, eventually you'll make progress.

BARACK OBAMA

WEEK 7: CHOOSE YOUR GOAL

Choose one item from TASK 1 which you want to address. Tick which type it is, then briefly write what it is in the box below.

□ Situation □ Person □ Aspect of Myself □ Value/Belief/Opinion

Write down the way(s) in which you DARE it by Denying, Avoiding, Repressing, or Excluding

I DENY this when I…	I AVOID this when I…
I REPRESS this when I…	I EXCLUDE this when I…

Dissect the details of *why* you can't accept this person/situation. Continue on more paper if you need to.

Grieve the expectations you had about this situation, person or aspect of yourself. You may want to write notes down here. Remember: it's normal to also feel grief for something you've never had or can never have.

Decide to fully accept some or all aspects of this situation/person/ aspect of yourself from today onwards, until you are ready to do things differently.:

Plan to move forward without letting it affect you negatively anymore.

To help me with this, I may need to:

Monday **Date:**

Overall I am feeling: 1 2 3 4 5 6 7 8 9 10

Through acceptance, I realise:

For self-care, I will / I did:

Going forward, I choose to:

Tuesday

Overall I am feeling: 1 2 3 4 5 6 7 8 9 10

Through acceptance, I realise:

For self-care, I will / I did:

Going forward, I choose to:

Wednesday

Overall I am feeling: 1 2 3 4 5 6 7 8 9 10

Through acceptance, I realise:

For self-care, I will / I did:

Going forward, I choose to:

Thursday

Overall I am feeling: 1 2 3 4 5 6 7 8 9 10

Through acceptance, I realise:

For self-care, I will / I did:

Going forward, I choose to:

Friday

Overall I am feeling: 1 2 3 4 5 6 7 8 9 10

Through acceptance, I realise:

For self-care, I will / I did:

Going forward, I choose to:

Saturday

Overall I am feeling: 1 2 3 4 5 6 7 8 9 10

Through acceptance, I realise:

For self-care, I will / I did:

Going forward, I choose to:

Sunday

Overall I am feeling: 1 2 3 4 5 6 7 8 9 10

Through acceptance, I realise:

For self-care, I will / I did:

Going forward, I choose to:

My notes:

Acceptance looks like a passive state but in reality, it brings something entirely new into this world. That peace, a subtle energy vibration, is consciousness.

ECKHART TOLLE, PHILOSOPHER

WEEK 8: CHOOSE YOUR GOAL

Choose one item from TASK 1 which you want to address. Tick which type it is, then briefly write what it is in the box below.

□ Situation □ Person □ Aspect of Myself □ Value/Belief/Opinion

Write down the way(s) in which you DARE it by Denying, Avoiding, Repressing, or Excluding

I DENY this when I…	I AVOID this when I…
I REPRESS this when I…	I EXCLUDE this when I…

Dissect the details of *why* you can't accept this person/situation. Continue on more paper if you need to.

Grieve the expectations you had about this situation, person or aspect of yourself. You may want to write notes down here. Remember: it's normal to also feel grief for something you've never had or can never have.

Decide to fully accept some or all aspects of this situation/person/ aspect of yourself from today onwards, until you are ready to do things differently.:

Plan to move forward without letting it affect you negatively anymore.

To help me with this, I may need to:

Monday **Date:**

Overall I am feeling: 1 2 3 4 5 6 7 8 9 10

Through acceptance, I realise:

For self-care, I will / I did:

Going forward, I choose to:

Tuesday

Overall I am feeling: 1 2 3 4 5 6 7 8 9 10

Through acceptance, I realise:

For self-care, I will / I did:

Going forward, I choose to:

Wednesday

Overall I am feeling: 1 2 3 4 5 6 7 8 9 10

Through acceptance, I realise:

For self-care, I will / I did:

Going forward, I choose to:

Thursday

Overall I am feeling: 1 2 3 4 5 6 7 8 9 10

Through acceptance, I realise:

For self-care, I will / I did:

Going forward, I choose to:

Friday

Overall I am feeling: 1 2 3 4 5 6 7 8 9 10

Through acceptance, I realise:

For self-care, I will / I did:

Going forward, I choose to:

Saturday

Overall I am feeling: 1 2 3 4 5 6 7 8 9 10

Through acceptance, I realise:

For self-care, I will / I did:

Going forward, I choose to:

Sunday

Overall I am feeling: 1 2 3 4 5 6 7 8 9 10

Through acceptance, I realise: ____________________

For self-care, I will / I did: ____________________

Going forward, I choose to: ____________________

My notes: ____________________

Understanding is the first step to acceptance, and only with acceptance can there be recovery.

J. K ROWLING, AUTHOR

8 WEEKS: YOU'VE DONE IT!

Eight weeks done! Congratulations on completing your journal!

The single most important thing you can do now is to *look back* and make a conscious effort to review your achievements over those 8 weeks.

When you started this journal, you became aware of situations, people, beliefs and aspects of yourself which you did not accept – and you wanted to be more accepting more of the time.

Go back to page 8 and take a detailed look at your Wheel of Life. Think about how you felt when you completed it and what you wanted to work towards.

Now complete a new Wheel of Life (overleaf), from how you feel *today*. This is an opportunity for you to notice any similarities and differences from when you completed it 8 weeks ago, and it is also a chance to ask yourself some questions.

MY WHEEL OF ACCEPTANCE (TAKE TWO)

COMPLETED ON:_______________

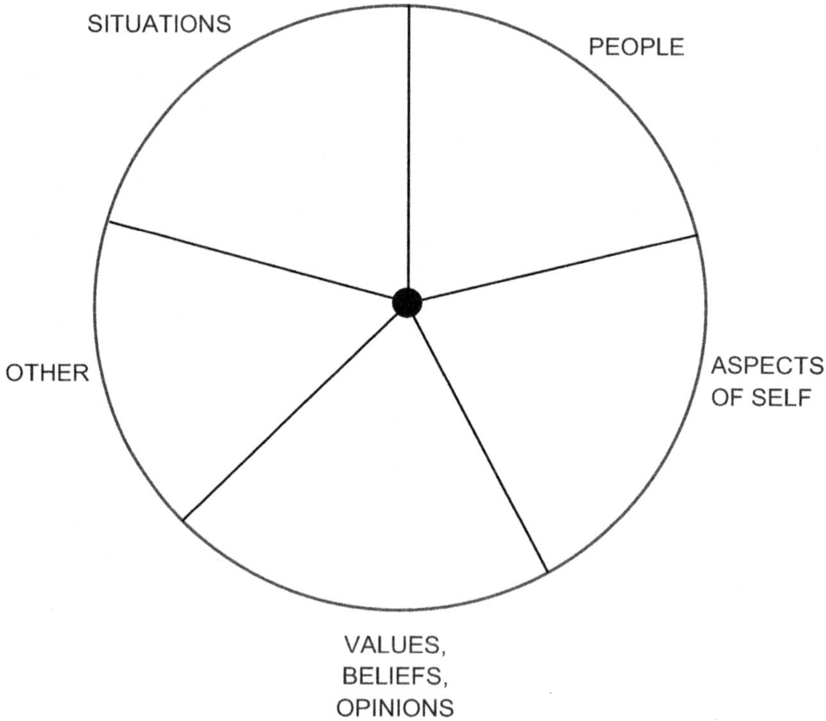

What has changed?

What has stayed the same?

What do you now find easier to accept?

Which areas will you keep working on?

What has been the best part of this process?

What have you found difficult?

What are you going to take from this process?

If you haven't quite reached one or more of your aims, now is not the time to give up. Continue to focus on those areas once completed, set yourself some new ones!

To continue with your journaling, there are many options out there including bullet journals, diaries, guided journals, quote-a-day diaries and also apps for your device. Have a look around and on the app stores to find the right one(s) for you…or buy another one of these!

Whatever you choose to do next, remember to keep checking back to remind yourself how far you have come.

Good luck with the next part of your journey and thank you for choosing to use this journal.

AND FINALLY

Thought colouring in was just for kids? It requires both sides of the brain. While logic helps you keep inside the lines, choosing your colours needs creativity, so it can be a great way to relax your mind and give yourself a well-earned break.

So grab yourself some coloured pencils and have a go on this mandala.

ABOUT THE AUTHOR

Katy Sheridan, together with her husband Dave, established Maximum Edge CIC after identifying significant gaps in provision of life-skills training which improve both mental and physical health.

Their combined professional experience across different sectors has helped them to develop bespoke training programmes which challenge, motivate, educate and encourage individuals to unlock their potential and that of the people around them.

They bring their expertise to numerous companies and organisations to assist in the development of people – from service users to managing directors and everyone in between.

For more information, please visit www.maximumedge.org.uk

Acceptance of differences is the first step to understanding.
SWAMI SIVANANDA

Printed in Great Britain
by Amazon

36818054R00056